WALKABOUT
Under the Ground

KT-555-705

This edition 2003

Franklin Watts
96 Leonard Street
London EC2A 4XD

Franklin Watts Australia
45-51 Huntley Street
Alexandria
NSW 2015

Copyright © 1993 Franklin Watts
Editor: Ambreen Husain
Design: Volume One

All rights reserved. No part of this publication may be reproduced, stored in a retrieval system, or transmitted in any form or by any means, electronic, mechanical, photocopy, recording or otherwise, without the prior written permission of the copyright owner.

A CIP catalogue record for this book is available from the British Library.

ISBN: 0 7496 5266 7

Printed in Hong Kong/China

Photographs: Bruce Coleman Ltd (A J Purcell) 17, (J Burton) cover, 18, (G Dore) 20, (J & D McClurg) 21; Eye Ubiquitous 26, 27 inset, 28; Chris Fairclough/Franklin Watts 6; Robert Harding 23, 29 inset; NHPA (G I Bernard) 7, (M Grey) 19; Oxford Scientific Films (G I Bernard) 14, (R Redfern) 15; Q.A. Photos Ltd 24; Survival Anglia (M Tibbles) 12, (F Furlong) 13; ZEFA 16, 22, 25, 27, 29, 30, 31.

Additional photographs: Stephen Oliver

WALKABOUT
Under the Ground

Henry Pluckrose

W
FRANKLIN WATTS
LONDON•SYDNEY

When you walk along
do you ever think
of the ground
beneath your feet?

The plants you tread on
have roots
which push down into the soil.
The roots carry food and water
to the plant.

Soil is mostly made of
tiny pieces of broken rock.
Dead plants and animals rot
and mix with the rock
to form soil.
Does all soil look the same?

Many creatures
live in the soil.
Woodlice like to live
in damp soil.

Worms tunnel through the soil
and make spaces
for air and water.

Farmers and gardeners
use the soil to grow crops
and garden plants.
They make holes in the soil
for seeds.

Many of the vegetables we eat grow beneath the ground.

Many animals burrow into the soil to make their homes. Burrows are safe places to live because enemies find it difficult to get inside. Rabbits live underground in large groups. Their underground home is called a warren.

Rabbits usually spend the day
underground and come out
in the evening to feed.
Every warren has several
entrances.

The fox lives in a hole called an earth.

Tree roots make a strong, safe roof and long tunnels lead to its secret entrances.

Moles live below ground too.
They burrow through the soil
looking for things to eat.
Sometimes their burrow
reaches ground level.

Molehills are
the little heaps of earth
pushed up by moles.

Water voles live in burrows along the banks of rivers. They feed on the soft plants which grow in the wet soil of the river bank.

Even birds build nests
below the ground.
A pair of kingfishers
have built their nest
in a steep river bank.
They catch the fish
which live in the river.

Some streams run underground
before they appear
at ground level.
Rainwater soaks down
into underground rocks.
Over many years, the water
wears away some of the rock
making passages and caves.

Some people like to explore underground passages and caves. They wear special clothes and carry powerful torches when they explore.

Some people work underground... like these miners digging for coal.

Engineers work underground
to cut tunnels
through the earth.
To make it easy
for travellers
tunnels are built
through mountains...

and even through the earth beneath the sea.

In some big cities
trains travel underground.

There are many other things
beneath the pavement.
You can see some of them
when you look down
into a workman's hole.

There are cables for
electricity
and telephones,
pipes for gas and water.

We dig into the ground to make the foundations for buildings.

The remains of houses,
old coins and broken pots
lie buried in the ground.
We may find clues
to tell us how people lived
hundreds of years ago.

Think of all the things
which live and grow
in the ground beneath your feet.

People use the ground
in many ways.
We must be careful how we use it.

About this book

Young children acquire much information in an incidental, almost random fashion. Indeed, they learn much just by being alive! The books in this series complement the way in which young children learn. Through photographs and a simple text the readers are encouraged to comment on the world in which they live.

To the young child, life is new and almost everything in the world is of interest. But interest alone is not enough. If a child is to grow intellectually this interest has to be harnessed and extended. This book adopts a well tried and successful method of achieving this end. By focusing upon a particular topic, it invites the reader firstly to look and then to question. The words and photographs provide a starting point for discussion. Discussion also involves listening. The adult who listens to the young reader's observations will quickly realise that children have a very real concern for the environmental issues that confront us all.

Children enjoy having information books read to them just as much as stories and poetry. The younger child may ignore the written words ... pictures play an important part in learning, particularly if they encourage talk and visual discrimination.

Henry Pluckrose